FIGHTER JET

Lisa Trumbauer

Raintree

Chicago, Illinois

© 2008 Raintree
Published by Raintree,
A division of Reed Elsevier Inc.
Chicago, Illinois

Customer Service 888-454-2279

Visit our website at www.heinemannraintree.com

Designed by Philippa Jenkins and Q2A Creative

Printed and bound in China by Leo Paper Group

12 11 10 09 08
10 9 8 7 6 5 4 3 2 1

**Library of Congress Cataloging-in-Publication
Data**
Trumbauer, Lisa
  Fighter jet / Lisa Trumbauer.
  p. cm.
  Includes bibliographical references and index.
  ISBN-13: 978-1-4109-2852-8 (lib. bdg.)
  ISBN-10: 1-4109-2852-7 (lib. bdg.)
 -- ISBN-13: 978-1-4109-2869-6 (pbk.)
  ISBN-10: 1-4109-2869-1 (pbk.)
1. Matter--Properties--Juvenile literature.
2. Fighter planes--Design and construction--Juvenile
literature. I. Title.
  QC173.36.T78 2007
  530.4--dc22
                                    2007003100

Acknowledgments
The author and publisher are grateful to the
following for permission to reproduce copyright
material: Corbis pp. **5**, **8**, **9**, **14**, **28** (George Hall),
6–7 (Philip Wallick), **18**; Corbis/Aero Graphics,
Inc./ p. **21** (Randy Jolly) [Lockheed]; Corbis/CNP
p. **16** (Steve White); Corbis/epa p. **12–13** (Benoit
Doppagne); Corbis/Reuters p. **26** (Arnd Wiegmann);
Getty Images/Hulton Archive p. **11**; US Air Force pp.
19 (Tech. Sgt. Ben Bloker), **23**, **25** (Master Sgt. Val
Gempis).

Cover photograph of a McDonnell Douglas F-15A
Eagle Jet Fighter reproduced with permission of
Corbis/George Hall.

Illustrations by Mark Preston.

The publishers would like to thank Nancy Harris and
Harold Pratt for their assistance in the preparation of
this book.

Disclaimer
All the Internet addresses (URLs) given in this book
were valid at the time of going to press. However,
due to the dynamic nature of the Internet, some
addresses may have changed, or sites may have
changed or ceased to exist since publication. While
the author and publishers regret any inconvenience
this may cause readers, no responsibility for any such
changes can be accepted by either the author or the
publishers.

It is recommended that adults supervise children on
the Internet.

Contents

Some words are printed in bold, **like this**. You can find out what they mean on page 30. You can also look in the box at the bottom of the page where they first appear.

Ready, Jet, Go!

Look! Up in the sky! What is that thing zooming overhead? It is a special type of airplane. It is a fighter jet!

The army uses fighter jets. So does the air force. Fighter jets are used in battle. They can travel much faster than other planes. They can make sudden moves. They can make tight turns in the air. They are built to be very strong. Fighter jets are built to be better and faster than any other plane.

This fighter jet is an F-15. They are also called F-15 Eagles.

F-15 facts

Type of Jet: F-15

How fast can it go?
- 1,875 miles per hour (3,017 kilometers per hour)

How high can it fly?
- 65,000 feet (19,812 meters)

How many people fly it?
- 1 or 2

How wide is it from wing to wing?
- 42.8 feet (13 meters)

How long is it?
- 63.8 feet (19.4 meters)

Everything Matters

Fighter jets are not simple machines. They have many parts. Some parts, like the wings, help the plane fly up and down. Other parts help the plane steer. The engine gives the fighter jet the power to zoom forward.

All these different parts have something in common. They are all made of **matter**. Matter is anything that takes up space. The form matter takes is called its **state**. Some matter is hard, like wood. Some matter is liquid, like water. Some matter is not easy to see because it is a gas, like air.

Most parts on a fighter jet are solid. Solids keep their shape. They only change shape when something changes them.

Imagine you could tap the side of this fighter jet. What would it feel like? You cannot move your hand through it. The outside of a fighter jet is solid matter.

matter anything that takes up space and can be weighed
oxygen gas that most living things breathe
state form of matter

What's the matter?

You probably already know some examples of the states of matter.

Solids: wood, stones, plastics

Liquids: water, juices, gasoline, oil

Gases: **oxygen** (the air we breathe), helium (gas used in balloons)

Fueled up

Cars need **fuel** to make them go. So do fighter jets. Fighter jets use a special jet fuel. The jet fuel is liquid. Liquid is a **state** (form) of **matter**. Solids keep their shape. Liquids do not. A liquid's shape changes to fit the space it is in.

Like all liquids, the jet fuel's shape changes. First, the fuel is the shape of the fuel tank. Then, it flows into the hose. It becomes the shape of the hose. Finally, the fuel flows into the fighter jet's fuel tank. The fuel is now the shape of the fuel tank.

hose

A fighter jet uses up a lot of fuel when it flies at top speed. See the hose? This fighter jet is refueled in midair!

Oxygen spreads out inside an oxygen tank. It spreads out inside the pilot's lungs, too.

Fighter pilots often wear **oxygen** masks. Oxygen is a gas we breathe. Gas is a state of matter. Some gases are hard to see and feel. Gases spread out to fill up the space they are in. The air we breathe is made of gases.

Designing Airplanes

When people make new things, they think about **matter**. They think about whether they can use solids, liquids, or gases.

They think about the **properties** (features) of matter. They think about how matter changes. For example, can a substance bend easily? Is it hard or soft? Does it break or burn? These are all properties of matter.

People think about matter when they **design** (make plans for) airplanes. The first fighter planes were flown during World War I (1914–1918). They were made of wood. Wood is hard. It cannot bend without breaking. However, wood burns easily. Burning easily is not good for a fighter plane!

Light weights

Wood and cloth are not as strong as some other solids, but they are light. During World War I, airplane engines did not have a lot of power. So, planes could not be too heavy. A wooden airplane was light enough to fly.

design draw plans for something

The first fighter planes were made of wood and cloth. Cloth is a solid. It is a soft solid.

Make mine metal

Airplane designers kept trying new ideas. In World War I, they started to think about using **metal**. Metal is a solid. It is hard, like wood. Unlike wood, metal does not burn easily. It does not break easily. It is strong. Most metals are also shiny. Metal can be made into different shapes.

metal hard substance that is usually shiny

Airplane designers thought metal would be great for airplanes. They could make the metal into an airplane's shape. The metal would not catch fire. It would not break easily. Metal can be heavier than wood, but that was okay. Airplane designers had built stronger engines.

Today, modern fighter jets have many metal parts. They also have parts made of other materials.

The Supermarine Spitfire was flown during World War II (1939–1945). It looks different from the World War I fighter planes.

Metal matters

There is more than one type of metal. Most metals have similar **properties** (features). Most metals are strong. Copper, lead, and gold are all metals.

Break It Down

A fighter jet is made of many parts. The **fuselage** is the main body of the jet. The tip of the fuselage is called the nose. The wings are attached to the fuselage. So are the tail and the engines. All these parts are made of **matter**.

Like the fighter jet, matter is made up of smaller parts. These smaller parts are called **atoms**. Atoms are so tiny that we cannot see them. Billions and billions of atoms join together. They form matter that we can see. The atoms have **properties** (features).

The atoms of different **metals** are different. Iron atoms are different from aluminum atoms. That is why different kinds of matter have different properties.

It takes billions and billions of atoms to make a fighter jet. Its parts are made of many different types of atoms.

weapons/missiles

atom tiny building block for all living things
fuselage main body of an airplane

Try again!

The F-15 fighter jet is always being improved. The very first one, the F-15A, was built in 1972. Better F-15 jets are now being flown.

fuselage

fuel tank

nose

Even the cockpit of a fighter jet is made up of smaller parts.

electron particle that moves around the center (nucleus) of an atom
neutron neutral particle found in the center (nucleus) of an atom
nucleus center section of an atom
proton positive particle found in the center (nucleus) of an atom

Look inside

Each part of the fighter jet is made up of even smaller parts. Look inside the cockpit of an F-15. There are a lot of parts. There are many controls. They help the pilot fly the airplane.

If you looked inside an **atom**, you would also see smaller parts. Of course, it is impossible for us to look inside an atom. Atoms are much too tiny to see. The parts of an atom are even smaller!

The center of the atom is called the **nucleus**. The nucleus is made up of **particles** (parts). These particles are called **protons** and **neutrons**. There are also particles called **electrons**. Electrons move around the nucleus.

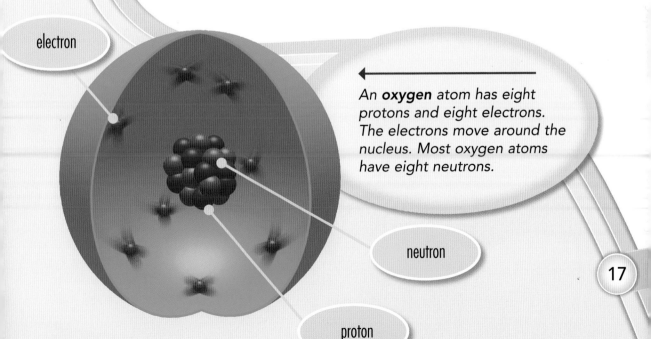

electron

*An **oxygen** atom has eight protons and eight electrons. The electrons move around the nucleus. Most oxygen atoms have eight neutrons.*

neutron

proton

17

Different particles

All **atoms** (tiny building blocks) are made of **particles** (parts). These particles are called **electrons**, **protons**, and **neutrons**. These particles are always the same. They never change. It is only the number of particles that changes. Different kinds of atoms have a different number of protons.

Everyday metal

Do you ever use aluminum foil? Aluminum is an element. It is a **metal**. But aluminum is different from iron. Aluminum is different because its atoms have a different number of protons.

Iron and copper are different elements. But they are both metals. Copper is used to make wires.

element substance that contains only one type of atom

For example, the outside of a fighter jet might be made of iron. An iron atom has 26 protons. Wires inside the jet are made of copper. A copper atom has 29 protons. Iron and copper have different **properties** (features). They are different **elements**. An element is a substance that contains only one type of atom.

↑ The fighter jet has a sleek shape. This shape helps it fly smoothly through the air.

The Stealth Jet

This fighter jet is a special kind. It is the F-117 Nighthawk. It is a **stealth** fighter. That means that it is hard for machines to **detect** (find) it.

The Nighthawk's surface is made of many different materials. One of these is called titanium. Like iron and copper, titanium is an **element**. An element is made of only one kind of **atom** (tiny building block). All the atoms in titanium are titanium atoms.

It's element–al!

Scientists have found more than 100 elements. You have probably heard of some of them. Helium and calcium are elements.

Each element is different. But all elements have one thing in common. Each element is made of only one type of atom.

A stealth fighter jet has straight sides. A regular fighter jet has curved sides.

Make it disappear

Engineers worked a long time to **design** the **stealth** bomber. Engineers are scientists who design and make things. They wanted to build a fighter jet that was nearly invisible. They wanted it to be hard to find.

Most jets can be **detected** (seen) by **radar**. Radar sends out invisible waves. The waves bounce off an object. The waves are measured. Radar helps to find objects that are far away.

Engineers wanted the stealth fighter to have a special kind of skin. The skin could not be detected by radar. The skin was made of **atoms** and **molecules**. A molecule is made up of two or more atoms joined together.

The blips on the radar screen tell people that an aircraft is nearby.

Atoms in pairs

Atoms join with other atoms to make molecules. Some molecules are made up of the same type of atom. For example, an **oxygen** atom can join with another oxygen atom. The two atoms form a molecule.

engineer person who uses science to make or improve something
molecule two or more atoms joined together
radar device that sends out invisible waves and records when the...

These two oxygen atoms have joined together. They have formed a molecule.

Stealth science

An **element** is made of only one kind of **atom** (tiny building block). Some things are made of more than one element.

Two of the same type of atoms can join to form a **molecule**. It is still an element. But molecules can be made from different kinds of atoms. Two or more elements can combine. They make a **compound**. Water is a compound. Each water molecule has one **oxygen** atom and two hydrogen atoms. Water is made from two elements, oxygen and hydrogen.

For the **stealth** fighter, **engineers** tried out different compounds. A compound's **properties** (features) are different from the properties of the original elements. For example, oxygen and hydrogen are gases. Water is liquid. Its properties are different.

Finally, the engineers found the right compound for the stealth bomber's skin. It made the stealth bomber invisible to **radar**!

Stealth secret!

The stealth fighter is made up of elements and compounds. The exact combination of the skin is a secret!

absorb soak up
compound combination of two or more elements

Jets in Action

These **stealth** fighters are examples of **atoms** in action. Without atoms and **molecules**, there would be no stealth jets. There would be no fighter jets at all!

A stealth fighter can fly at 684 miles per hour (1,100 kilometers per hour).

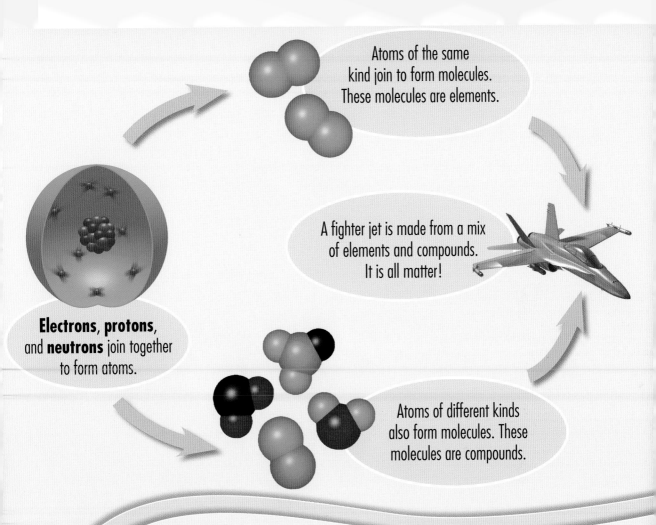

Atoms of the same kind join to form molecules. These molecules are elements.

A fighter jet is made from a mix of elements and compounds. It is all matter!

Electrons, protons, and neutrons join together to form atoms.

Atoms of different kinds also form molecules. These molecules are compounds.

Everything on Earth is made of **matter**. That means everything is made of atoms. Matter can be an **element**, like iron. An element is made of only one type of atom. Matter can be a **compound**, like water. A compound is a combination of two or more elements. Matter can be solid, like the frame of a fighter jet. It can be liquid, like jet **fuel**. It can be a gas, like the air we breathe.

27

Stealth Matters

Look at this jet. Where would you find each **state** of **matter** listed below?

1. a solid, like **metal**
2. a liquid, like jet **fuel**
3. a gas, like **oxygen**

The cockpit is covered with special material. The material hides the pilot inside! **Radar** will not bounce off the pilot's curved helmet.

Most jet engines give off heat. Some missiles seek out heat to find their target. They will not find the **stealth** jet! These thin slots spread out the heat. That makes the stealth harder to find.

Stealth facts

Type of jet: F-117 Stealth fighter

- Top speed: 684 mph (1,100 kph)
- Range (on one tank of fuel): 500 miles (805 kilometers)

- Weight: 52,500 pounds (23,813 kilograms)
- Width (wing to wing): 43 feet 4 inches (13.3 meters)
- Length: 65 feet 11 inches (20.3 meters)

The sides of the plane are flat.

The tail is shaped like a V. On most planes, the tail moves. Not on the stealth jet!

Answers:
1. The main body of the jet is a solid.
2. The fuel tank contains liquid fuel.
3. Inside the cockpit, the pilot breathes gases in the air.

Glossary

absorb soak up. A sponge can absorb water.

atom tiny building block for all living things. A fighter jet is made of billions and billions of atoms.

compound combination of two or more elements. Water is a compound made from oxygen and hydrogen.

design draw plans for something. It takes a lot of work to design an airplane.

detect see or find something. Radar can detect most airplanes.

electron particle that moves around the center (nucleus) of an atom. Electrons are incredibly tiny.

element substance that contains only one type of atom. All living and nonliving things are made of elements.

engineer person who uses science to make or improve something. Some engineers design aircraft.

fuel something that is burned to make heat or power. Fighter jets use a special type of jet fuel.

fuselage main body of an airplane. A plane's wings are attached to the fuselage.

matter anything that takes up space and can be weighed. Everything on Earth is made of matter.

metal hard substance that is usually shiny. Iron, copper, and titanium are metals.

molecule two or more atoms joined together. A molecule of water has two hydrogen atoms and one oxygen atom.

neutron neutral particle found in the center (nucleus) of an atom. Most oxygen atoms have eight neutrons.

nucleus center section of an atom. Protons and neutrons are found in the nucleus.

oxygen gas that most living things breathe. Oxygen is an element.

particle tiny part of something. Atoms are the smallest particles of matter.

property special feature of different types of matter. A substance's hardness is one of its properties.

proton positive particle found in the center (nucleus) of an atom. An iron atom has 26 protons.

radar device that sends out invisible waves and records when they bounce back. Radar can be used to find airplanes far away.

state form of matter. Solid, liquid, and gas are all states of matter.

stealth secret, or hard to see. The stealth fighter is made of special compounds.

Want to Know More?

Books to read

- Green, Michael and Gladys. *War Planes: Stealth Attack Fighters: The F-117A Nighthawks*. Mankato, MN: Capstone, 2003.

- Stone, Lynn. *Fighting Forces in the Air: F-15 Eagle*. Vero Beach, FL: Rourke, 2004.

- Spilsbury, Louise and Richard. *Atoms and Molecules*. Chicago: Heinemann Library, 2007.

Websites

- http://education.jlab.org/atomtour
  Learn more about atoms and their tiny parts.
- http://www.af.mil/factsheets
  Click on links on the right to find out more about the jets in this book.

Read more about matter and its properties in *A Matter of Survival*.

Find out about odd states of matter in *State of Confusion*.

Index